"Rob Jacques shares my love of interior dance that expresses itself in words—too shy for the dance floor, but not for the page. I'm not surprised we were born on the same day."

Bill Porter
author of *Finding Them Gone:*
Visiting China's Poets of the Past

"Rob Jacques hears thousand-year-old voices of Chinese poets and responds with new songs and harmonies. His works are beautiful testaments to poetic connection and the contemplation of space, body, and mind."

Deng Ming-Dao
author of *365 Tao*

"When Einstein taught us that energy equals mass times the speed of light squared, he was projecting a sacred truth against the veil of life. In *Adagio for Su Tung-p'o*, Rob Jacques invokes the masters of ancient Chinese poetry to pull back that veil and illuminate the concepts of time, presence, love, memory, and even physical death. For all its quiet moments of observation and contemplation, this book is a big bang. The epigraphs themselves connect the spaces between the stars and are worthy of a stand-alone read. When those epigraphs become passages into the physics and metaphysics of Jacques' own existence—a life well-lived and the sparks and spirits having carried that life—*Adagio* takes on a form and genre all its own. Part spiritual autobiography, part homage to timeless poetry, and part blueprint to quiet the noise—or at least to give it a closer listen—Rob Jacques has blurred and crossed all the lines, which, in a paradox Su Tung-p'o would have loved, makes the beauty of simply being crystal clear."

Bryan Borland
author of *DIG*

"At this fraught political moment, *Adagio for Su Tung-p'o* is like one long centering prayer spoken for the soul of the world. Read Rob Jacques' deeply-mined meditations slowly, one by one, until you feel your own consciousness uplifted by these 'orchestrations of space and time and death . . . revealing a metaphysical purpose for breath.' His poems show us those deepest truths 'in between life's arias and wails' by looking head-on at the endless back-and-forth of the human mind with undeniable humility and precision."

James Crews
author of *Telling My Father*

"Rob Jacques's poems take us on a monk's journey toward discovery, holding up to the light the ways in which the material world fails us. Desire, love, youth, aging, death—these poems ask: what withers away, what remains? The poems in *Adagio for Su Tung-p'o* each open with an excerpt as a way to spur their thinking, and Jacques examines the metaphysical with wisdom, nostalgia, and grace. By engaging with these poetic sources, Jacques finds connection and revelation by calling back to Su Tung-p'o through a lyric history in order to, through language, close that distance."

Jacques J. Rancourt
author of *Novena*

Adagio for Su Tung-p'o

Poems on How Consciousness Uses Flesh
to Float Through Space/Time

Rob Jacques

Fernwood
PRESS

Adagio for Su Tung-p'o

Fernwood Press
Newberg, Oregon
www.fernwoodpress.com

Printed in the United States of America

Cover and interior layout and design: Mareesa Fawver Moss

Cover art: Sharosh Rajasekher

ISBN 978-1-59498-065-7

I respectfully and humbly dedicate this book to:

Burton Watson
Lin Yutang
Bill Porter / Red Pine
David Hawks
David Hinton

without whose sparkling and profound translations of
ancient Chinese text much vital humanity and philosophy would be
unknown to Western civilization.

Contents

Preface

Fortunately, no political borders or boundaries can stop ideas. Humans may erect all kinds of walls to keep other humans away and draw all kinds of red lines in the sand to warn other humans not to come any nearer, but those walls and lines are drivel that wind and water will erode and erase over time along with the governments that made them.

History has shown that no country (let alone religion, culture, or system of laws) lasts forever, for change and chaos come to all of them regardless of their size, economic accomplishments, military strength, or technological achievements.

But ideas, best expressed in art, stay strong and true, communicating clearly across civilization-destroying apocalypses to generations removed millennia from their humble creation. Ideas never age. A thought is always as fresh as the day it was first given form, even fresh on the day the dying planet on which it is housed becomes absorbed catastrophically by a reddening, expanding sun. Thoughts are our way of leaving our five senses behind so we may experience the metaphysical, something our flesh is incapable of knowing. Some call that experience, "using your imagination," or "dreaming." Fine.

Why quibble over semantics? Choose the term with which you are most comfortable, and then soar. Leave the physical world to teeter as it will, where it will, when it will, while your mind moves with quantum precision beyond the plane of the ecliptic and into dimensions science (for all its stupendous achievements) can only call oblivion. Science cannot know where you are going because science is bound by the material universe. Its reality is totally dependent on things, especially things that can be measured in numerous ways. Science is a tool of excellent value for our five senses, but in abstraction where you have gone, your five senses are worthless. Metaphysics (imagination, dreaming) is the tool you need now to study a reality apart from any reality you have studied before.

The ancient Chinese poets knew all this, and they positively loved ambiguity, loved paradox, and would have loved the puzzling, reality-defying entanglements that frustrate and fascinate quantum physicists today. They would have laughed at them, too, while exchanging good wine and poems with each other as they watched the moon rise and be reflected in the hundred rivers flowing through the thousand mountains surrounding them and all the ten thousand things.

Not that the ancient Chinese poets thought of metaphysics as a separate entity that dwelt apart from the everyday world of business, politics, family life, and daily living. Quite the opposite: they perceived themselves—and everyone else—as a consciousness flowing through time and space that was itself moving on a continuum ultimately both unknowable and unchangeable. They saw how useless (even if pleasurable) it was to amass things in the world, and things included titles, reputations, and power over others as well as wealth. The physical comforts these things afford the five senses are very real, indeed, but ultimately they have no staying power because their holders have no staying power either, and disease, disabilities, disillusionment, and death put an end to any enjoyment dependent on flesh. Yet in and around these comforting things are woven dimensions that can only be perceived by an intellect that has come to understand the connection between consciousness and nothingness, the relationship between materiality and emptiness, the bond between light and dark, terrestrial and celestial, being and nonbeing. We all flow aware and unaware through a many-tiered existence whose beginning is no better understood than its ending, but we can observe, meditate on, accept, and be uplifted by what we cannot change or even fathom. It's in that observing, meditating, and accepting that our consciousness is lifted up and out of mortal woe toward oblivion's restful and triumphant emptiness and immortality.

The ancient Chinese poets are worth our time. T'ao Ch'ien, Wang Wei, Li Bai, Du Fu, Han Shan, Wang An-shih, and a host of others who lived centuries ago already understood how thin the veneer of science and technology is, how easily it is rubbed away, and how profound the mystery is that flows just beneath it. They used their lifetimes to explore the companionship existing between the material and the immaterial, between the mortal and the immortal, between time and eternity, and they did so while participating in politics, commerce, travel, and mundane daily community life. But they knew the value of being awake and aware of infinity all around them, awake and aware of how insubstantial space/time is, how suddenly it can turn, and how its glitter is a mere refraction of a light not directly observable by the five senses of our flesh.

For example, take the situation of Su Tung-p'o. Born into a family of moderate means at the height of a militarily weak but artistically brilliant dynasty, Su Tung-p'o worked hard at his education and government job. A sensitive and politically savvy young man, he rose relatively quickly in the Sung bureaucracy and enjoyed participating in the usual rounds of policy-making, civil administration, and cultural arts. He felt secure in his job, saw his future bright, and believed his occasional forays into painting and writing poetry would enhance his reputation among his friends, co-workers, and superiors. He was wrong. After writing some poems that were interpreted by a few powerful Sung Dynasty courtiers as being critical of official policies and perhaps even anti-imperial, he found out how quickly the sweets of the material world can sour. It was at this point in his dramatically altered life that his poetry became a somewhat plaintive but very determined search for value and enlightenment, and that delicate, exploratory poetry has survived nine hundred years of human chaos and natural turbulence to come to us as an aid to our own journey toward wisdom.

So it is with deep humility and much gratitude that I take lines from Su Tung-p'o and a few other poets as epigraphs to produce an adagio, a slow and thoughtful progression through a theme—the only theme, actually, worth a lifetime: pursuing the metaphysical conjoining of life and love with eternity.

Rob Jacques
Autumn 2019

Adagio for Su Tung-p'o

When will we listen to the soft rustle of night rain?
You too know these things mustn't be forgotten.

—Su Tung-p'o

Nothing impeding falling rain, so down it comes
universally coating green, impassive mountains,
softly wetting bodies, relaxing fretting souls,
drenching a cooling earth, saturating still forests,
falling peacefully over fields and cities, falling
to wash clean night's cares, day's affairs, falling
to reinvigorate the tools of the Eight Immortals.

The steady rain falls like trillions of nanoseconds
from eternity, always more from whence they came,
always a plethora, a surfeit of raindrops wetting
our worlds, whetting our desires for companionship,
begetting our dreams of Paradise and Gomorrah,
the heady rain making us drunk on prophecies
of perfect places in perfect times lived perfectly.

What gods would we have? What good would they be?
The hundred rivers, the countless scudding clouds,
the ten thousand years would flow without regard
to orison or chant or song to wispy supreme beings
however strong the logic, magic, or religious cant
we use to bring them into our ken, however complex
our reasoning within the temporal minds of men.

Our daily routines, performed a millennium apart,
took and take no notice as the hundred rivers flow—
our eating and sleeping, our talking and kissing,
our silliness over accomplishing stuff, walking
and meeting others, missing this thing and that,
our willingness to forget and forgo: all camouflage
for our mortality that can turn warm rain to snow.

A millennium has flowed on, its years splashing
war and love, love and war, lives of the living,
ghosts of those gone, dashing hopes and fears
against rocks of the days and hours as it rode along
over endlessness and ceaselessness and hellos
and goodbyes, over appearances and disappearances
under evolving, revolving, devolving bottomless skies.

In our times, your hundred rivers still flow on,
your green hills range forever horizon-less on and on
with their future identical to their past, past and future
intermingled and intermingling both misty and timeless,
autumn and spring, spring and autumn leapfrogging
each other through numberless vales and dells where
can be heard the pure ring of echoing temple bells.

When will we pause? When will we release ourselves
to flow with ease to where Eden and Sodom dwell?
The old heart remembers where the young heart's been.
Old times are connected to new times by threads and
strings and ropes and chains and veins of experience
until experience expires and only innocence remains
from the multitudinous ashes of our fleshy desires.

Human officialdom has forgotten the forests,
busy with data and dicta, not noticing the rain,
the soft, soddening, simple rain still falling as we
make our way through hours and days toward
absence, and bureaucracies flourish in the mind,
imagine statistics, invent systems, come to find
at the end of their chimerical world nothing stays.

Absence is fallow ground for our imaginations,
absence the sustenance of desire, the substance
of wisdom, the *sine qua non* of creation, indivisible
and entire in and of itself, absence being ambience
to all things within space/time, absence being
source and goal, designer and designed, alluring
and luring to those of a philosophic frame of mind.

The narrow trail of trials rises up this mountain or that,
mountain after mountain in succession, narrow trail
ahead half hidden in mists as it rises, then descends
steeply, aimlessly, seamlessly, tracelessly into legend
where emptiness will prevail and sense depends
on quantum particles afloat, aloft, dreamlessly
asleep in both of us and in consciousnesses to come.

Imperfect memories lead to imperfect histories,
and our five senses, yours and mine, produce life's
merry heresies, gains and losses, fodder for miseries,
water and wine, produce illusion of being somewhere,
of accomplishment, of solving mysteries, our senses
leading us to belief in fortune, punishment and reward,
leading us to abandonment of all experience as fraud.

The slide of seasons through us disguises eternity's tide,
infinity's many immensities that the hundred rivers
wash downstream with us, around us, within us until
we disappear as light disappears, as night disappears,
our loves eddying in pools of elation and grief in our
hearts that grasp at reeds along the hundred rivers' banks,
as we and all brief things rush on through denial and belief.

We are no closer to each other than personal legends
allow, no farther apart than quarks, leptons, and bosons
in the here and now, space/time irrelevant in the reality
of the hundred rivers flowing on, you and I rolling along
through numerous gorges, over numberless cataracts,
ultimately out beyond the plane of the ecliptic
and into a perpetuity where the unknown throng.

Alone at night on your narrow trail from here to there,
alone at night moving in rain beneath unseen stars,
alone at night, just you and your cart, you in your robe,
did you think you were on an interminable journey,
you, letting the hundred rivers take you to where
all things eventually repair, becoming cognizant that
all things eventually are forgotten, tumble, and sink?

Alone at night in your hut, in my house, you, me,
alone together a millennium apart, do we think
of each other? Did you wonder where a river's flow
would bring us, you and me, far upstream-downstream
from each other? Was your night like mine? Alone
in going from oblivion to oblivion, did you know
that everything and therefore nothing is forever flown?

Love, noun and verb, Chinese inked brushstrokes
or American digital keystrokes, love alone touches,
feels, aches, yearns, satisfies us on the narrow trail
to elsewhere, as we ride along forward toward fate,
love alone lasting longer than the strongest power
humanly imaginable, love accompanying our going,
love, our only, lonely reason to see our lives as song.

Amor Fati

As evening clouds withdraw, a clear cool air floods in.
The jade wheel passes silently across the Silver River.
This life, this night, has rarely been kind.
Where will we see this moon next year?

—Su Tung p'o

As thoughts of mortality withdraw, look to the sky.
If unable to stand, then sit. If unable to sit, then lie.
Let the cool, clear air of reflection flood in to water
parched memories conjured in the mind's sepia eye.

Trace awe with the miraculous wand of imagination,
the silver river of the Milky Way floating galaxies
from the Big Bang toward oblivion. Trace the bond
among quantum particles that creates time and space.

This life, this night, mean no harm and are unkind
through indifference, not malevolence, and your flesh
is not a universe's trophy, nor should it be yours, for
in old age only love's experience keeps a mind fresh.

In another year, will we be able to see the moon?
Will either you or the moon still be here? Embrace
the obstacle. It's the way. It's the path of all travel,
learning pain, earning wisdom, then discerning grace.

Argument in a Time of Supremacists

How dare I express discontent in a time of peace?

—Su Tung-p'o

My body is at peace, but without my peace of mind.
My discontent arises from supremacists of every kind
who never cease to persecute advocates of open hearts
and borders. Indifferent nature advises cooperation
for survival, not isolation or attack. Am I the only one
who surmises imperial pique will end badly? How sad
supremacists lack civility, let alone love, for those who
seek relief from those of us who would offer it gladly.

I dare. I rise. I express myself boldly. I keep the faith
with all the other faithful, however few. I'd rather war
with thieves wracking decency and thugs lacking amity
in a war of words and ideas, keeping humanity at peace.
If I should stay in cold silence with you, I may seem
to be sleeping to supremacists who forever misconstrue.

Toward Metaphysics

too old for
vision I must
settle for dreams

—Keith Waldrop

When I was young, my head made plans
my body believed, for when I was callow,
my head controlled my quick, grabbing hands,
logic ruled, and space/time fooled me
into thinking order would lick life's chaos,
that misrule would succumb to a tide
of progress, to enlightenment, a new Eden
if we tried, if only tomorrow would come,

but now I'm old. My heart forgets lessons
taught in days of yore that came to nothing.
My heart now rules my opening hands as they
unclutch history, reach for dreams, and I,
letting go of the scientific method, flow on
a new reality that my imagination streams.

Hermit

the mist of loneliness dissolves
as our far-reaching spirits consider the sky

—Wei Ying-wu

I should come out of my cave, up from my depths,
away from my woods, apart of the desert of my desires
to see who won the last election, to hear dogma and dicta,
to be corrected, shamed, punished, infected, maligned,
to learn religion, pseudo-science, cultural ignominy,
military superiority, radical racist terrorism refined,
and achieve and achieve and achieve, measuring dross
as if it were other than possessions properly defined.

But loves are comfortable, erotic or otherwise, and they bring
joy in just being, in using all five senses for exploration,
adulation, adoration of a physical world heightened by
isolation of the mind, loves meekly seeking loves unfrightened
by hatreds, however many, to whatever degree unkind,
loves ineffable, ineluctable, inescapable, timeless and blind.

The world will not let me go, grabs my arm, grasps, grips,
gropes and tries to charm with its cyber devices and high-tech
encumbrances that, for all their glitter, all my hopes, have not
the balm of lips moist and slightly parted, have not the calm
unfolding at the glacial pace of the universe that symbolizes,
signifies, and sets the standard for a calm unfolding of myself
to make a place for metaphysics and infinity, to keep a space
apart for the soft, slow understanding of love as divinity.

I am alone. Language has left me bereft of communication,
and I am unable to explain my feeling of absence, but I am
on my own, and I harbor no regret, no recriminations, no
blame for others, for I am myself the wilderness through
which the world wanders afraid and trembling, my bliss
a forgetting, a turning, a renunciation, my kiss a flame.

Bedtime

for taking things away surreptitiously
nothing outdoes the night

—Su Tung-p'o

What remains, when all has gone eventually,
are quanta, and what better backdrop than dark?
God bless night. Too bad our sun isn't like
all other stars, too far from us to be too bright,
for sunlight deceives, creating in us the thought
that reality is what our physical eye believes.

The mind's eye, however, perceives best blind
in night's febrile dark, sight-thieving dark,
where one-by-one-by-one our thoughts unwind,
misshape, and evanesce, then disappear, leaving
blank our cerebellum as a holy place devoid
of dogma and dicta, both equally deceiving.

Surreptitiously does the night exercise its
prerogative like a sure lover, taking away
mental clothes ever so sweetly to reestablish
our innocence in sleep and hover over us
with all light gone, we, in oblivious bliss,
deep in dark, finding a taste of afterlife in this.

Come morning's resurrection, we begin again
to assemble day—that is to say, our lives. But
even in dawn, through morning and afternoon,
we know our lank, quotidian accumulations
will be taken away after evening's prayer, and
death-like, anonymous, night will be there,

and it will come to us with a stolid reliability,
a dependability, a philosophical inevitability,
a dark easing, erasing all we will into being,
and we spend 365 little mortalities unafraid,
each one finding night leaving us with nothing
the way death will, finally, light forever stayed.

Big Bang Theory of Love

I work to hold on to the night
while I can still brag I'm young.

—Su Tung-p'o

In my dark, I lie listening to soft night rain
incessant, infinite in its light ambience, and I
hark to water aloft on my roof, for I am adrift
abed in my effervescence where I've lain hot,
blood-sodden, hormone-trodden, aroused, ridden,
maddened by flesh, bidden endlessly to perform
lustily, pondering if it's inane, insane to treasure
pleasure in whomever and however it's housed.

When I wake, and at some point I know I will,
in my dying, will I go over the sill awaiting you?
For mercy's sake, let those powers that be anoint
you and me with vindication, for we were only
this: bowers for love's quantum particles afire,
effecting for an hour space/time's higher bliss.

Metaphysical Lessons

Almost all of this
is the mind editorializing
what the body does . . . .

—Sarah Anderson

Mind and body are inextricably linked
(actually extricably, because death is a device,
a cleaver, an unsplicer, that can extricate fact
from fiction in a trice) and though mind is obsessed
with body, oddly body can't care less about mind,
and unable to process metaphysical lessons, prefers
to mess around sensually, energetically, chaotically,
despotically, erotically with others of its kind.

Mind, trying to justify body's preoccupation with
things of the flesh in which it's housed, is distracted
from reality (which isn't physical) and about which body
is not aroused, but space and time conspire to wear
and age body into dissolution, body being an oddity
suffering anatomically through a deflation of desire
and a dementia that precludes possibility of body
exploring its relation to life except in absentia.

Mind rationalizes it all as if body were rational.
Body plays as if mortality didn't number its days.
Body plays with real bulls and dreamed unicorns
until it's gored, while mind's protective cautionings
are ignored. Hours are streamed into years, years
into scores before reality's truth is shown: nothing
we can sense exists, but what we think can be real,
and from those facts alone our universe is known.

Billy Surels

The hundred rivers day and night flow on,
we and all things following;
only the heart remains unmoved,
clutching the past.

—Su Tung-p'o

Who wouldn't clutch at a love that once glided past?
Even an early, long flown love that I knew wouldn't last
and for which I was shamed, shunned, derided.
The boy, dangerously beautiful, still stands cocky, sure,
his flannel shirt open, his lop-sided smile at coy play
with my heart, and he demands a memory or two. Even
at this remove, all my life has not been enough to inure
against remembrance of his eyes, lips, and callow voice.

This ill and old, this far downstream, what should I do?
Forget? Oblivion may be a wise choice for all that's past,
but I will hold on my departing day a recall of a first taste
of vanity and uncanny bliss, leaving behind the waste
of space and time, but cleaving to a lovely thing that also
couldn't last, clutching my evanescing memory of his kiss.

Candlelight

The east wind gently spreads her celestial glow.
The moon slips behind her veil of perfumed mist.
Afraid this flower won't stay up much longer,
I light a tall candle to view her crimson face.

                                        —Su Tung-p'o

Short candles are good for a moment's viewing,
but it takes a tall candle to keep watch a long time,
for when you've been abandoned by the moon
and light has vanished in the night's wild brewing,
only a tall candle lasts you through to dawn's sublime
eastern glow and everything coming to you under the sun,
and everything night has cloaked is now soaked in shine
and you can put away candles, for the dark is undone.

But the burning radiance of bright daylight makes
all things common, all things valued the same, unlike
the worth given to the candle's small circle of brilliance
lit before you in which your happiness is given birth,
a treasured face kept out of the saddening dark in
a measured space holier than anything else on earth.

Metaphysical Lesson № 1

letting go of sorrow returns us to wisdom
seeing the inner pattern ends attachment

—Hsieh Ling-yün

Release and ease yourself into forgoing grief
as best you can, when you can, throwing over
odd emotions that can in no way bring relief.

Love you thought you lost you have not lost,
though it will not appear in answer to your cry
even in your passions now storm-tossed, severe.

Fold your mind's wings, for this flight is done,
and bring to rest every pain you fear, for night
is not evil, nor is day good. You judge in vain.

Relax into nothing. Unwind. The time is right
for sloughing off snows building on your mind
where so long ago your slight innocence froze.

Empty yourself. Be conscious of nothing before
or after the fact of your being, laying down
burdens of scholarship and histories of yore

where religions arose and attached you to Earth,
convinced you civilizations were progress,
and every natural thing belonged to you at birth.

Disconnect yourself now, the moment being rife
with an omnipresence of oblivion, omnipotence
of ignorance, and omniscience of reclusive life.

Death? Is it a question? Life? Does it answer?
Willingly go down into obliteration, fall silent,
kiss wisdom easing you from the world's thrall.

Little sorrowing one, say goodbye. To yourself.
Your old self. Say no more. All you have are
ashes and stars going to ashes in a quantum sky.

Casting Shadows

Layer upon layer on the alabaster terrace,
I tell the boy to sweep them up in vain:
just as the sun takes them all away
the full moon brings them back again.

—Su Tung p'o

Lazily, hazily, unhurried in unsullied chiaroscuro night
my world's shadows are laid down one upon another
by silver-sleek illuminations of a full moon, and
tall grass's shadows lie slack, dank over a black earth,
maple's less dark shadows sprawl on top of them
but beneath lighter shadows of fir and pine, all of which are,
in turn, under an old, slender shadow I know as mine;
shadow upon shadow, tone upon tone fleck the gravel path
with dark, the wooden stair, the white stone deck.

Ghosts of calm souls, they are, spreading insubstantially,
unalarmed, soundless as dreams flavoring a disturbed sleep,
each with its unspoken message, its unspeakable angst,
each lying quietly one upon the other, wavering,
furling, unfurling with passing breezes, a moving moon,
each as fragile as a kind thought, yet strong as night is long,
each a support for human paranoia, mortal fear, uneasy mind,
each susceptible to eradication by a passing cloud,
each reappearing like the ghost it is, a darkened shroud.

What would it profit anyone to attempt their disappearance?
Wait long enough, endure long enough, and the blinding sun
will clear away moonlight's detritus with shafts and shards
of garish brightness that stab and tear like broken glass,
the hellish sun evaporating ghosts of every kind, leaving
path and stair and deck spanking bright, and where sunlight
smacks down against an object, the blocked shadow
is unsubtle black, nothing more, the sun turning day
into erasure with acts of photons fired through space.

But the moon is empowered where the sun is not,
the moon reflective, passive, subjective where the sun is not,
and its shadows of varying weaknesses, graynesses, degrees
of dark are themselves mirrored in the indefinite mind
that sees how after daylight's disasters, night comes again,
time transpires, and once more reality fades to something
more profound, shadows and their ghostly silence pointing
toward an end, toward what we've known with imagination
will come of us eventually whatever else we may intend.

What Matters

You just came from my old village
so you know all about village affairs.
When you left, outside my window,
was it in bloom—that winter plum?

—Wang Wei

All human affairs trail off behind us
into dust, into a history-less abyss,
all our goals and cares meaningless
in the infinity of change, coming, going,
and there is no greater rapture than this:
in oblivion we will not miss what we miss.

Truth and falsehoods, politics and pleasures,
loves and pseudo-loves, adventures and
ordeals: they will sleep unwakeable, ever
fated to slumber on in their new non-being,
never thought of, tamed and sated with death,
finally not feeling, not knowing, not seeing.

Important to me, however, is a thrush's song
sung unhesitatingly in a metaphysical dark,
the wind through the least dandelion's head
that blows along parachuting seeds though
the parent plant be spent, the lilac's sky-blue,
purple-red panicles' soft, sweetening scent.

Important to me, however, are sun-gold
honey-locust trees giving up glory in the fall,
winter hazel in yellow bloom, winter told
in river ice and frosting breeze, hoary roads
slickly white where plodders unexpectedly
dance, and the stress of life begins to ease.

Important to me, however, is a smile of
recognition from an old friend, a blown kiss
from a long-ago love met by chance, a lone
star tracking winter through a last romance,
and through it all, an absence of myself
whose body is of the same worth as stone.

Recluse

I'm old and sick and free of worry:
Mind is the master of its own cures.

—Po Chü-i

Found dead last night, but imagine him here still:
another day of rumination, meditation, medication
until another evening of relishing being alone,
a status that enhances his stature, and he will
await with an old man's dedication dissolution
of blood and bone, whether it comes soon or late.

He has said his goodbyes to those worthy of them,
loved and lost his significant others along his way,
long ago stopped newspapers with their worldly cries
as he had gotten from them precious little news
of what matters metaphysically at the end of day,
differentiates those who win from those who lose.

Were he here now with you, nothing would change.
He'd be marking time, his experiences finished,
and he'd smile at you who are too young to know
what to make of small things become diminished,
items like possessions, acquaintanceships, and
civilizations newly pointless to one letting go.

Look where he might stand at his one window
were he here and not gone afield in the universe.
Pick up his half-drunk cup of coffee, his crumbs
from toast and jam, his used knife and spoon,
crumbled napkin and chipped china plate, things
allowing the old to proclaim against fate, "I am."

Against the wall rests his chair and a small stand.
Picture him there hour after hour reading his way
through classics and poems, writing now and then
a note or two to no one knowing worth and decay,
already well along toward oblivion's closure, he,
departing having done all required of old men.

Found dead last night, but imagine him content
to lay down life, space/time done, perhaps
a thought at the very last of a late love, perhaps
a feeling at the leaving gate of some one bliss
long past that stirs his mind, but nothing, really,
would you find that at his expiring he will miss.

Cumulus, Stratus, Cirrus

Through rain and shine, alternate night and day,
drifting at will and stopping as it may,
the cloud has made the universe its home.

—Su Tung-p'o

How long did it take me to learn all the dark,
its many forms and formulations, its shades
from warm grays to jet black, bold and stark,
from cloaking midnight in meadow glades
to a coating ebony hiding me in a city park,
from being groped and fondled in the theatre
to being wrestled down hot in a motel bed?

How long did it take me to learn all the light,
its many forms and formulations, its bright
assays into ecstasies of adolescent orgasms
to its essays on old age, chaste and contrite,
from its beacon of promise and revelation to
its candle of hope against corruption's might,
the sun, moon, and stars at the heart of sight?

Drifting at will through my life, stopping
to cope with my five senses or imagination,
wending where I may, ascending, descending,
I've found and lost fortunes, got and regretted
love, gained and shed youth and pride, until
I came awake and sustained an understanding
of space/time that made sport of human will.

Disappearance

Only make sure the mind never clings!

—Su Tung-p'o

Let metaphysics be the lubricant that slicks the mind
as it slips through time and space and comes to grips
with facts of passion and loss, facts of leaving behind
each life experience beyond imaginative memory's reach.

Employ the five senses to enjoy what flesh has to teach,
but remember aging condenses a life to a blip in eternity
when the grieving mind focuses on losses wisdom skips,
the mind loath to leaving even an old body's felicities.

How does one make the mind let go? Bring frost to roses,
ice to youth-strewn dreams. Let grass sleep beneath snow,
accept all that aging imposes. In spite of what it seems, all
passes in Cosmos' quantum particles' ebb and flow.

How does one take the mind away from the world? Let it
mourn awhile, and then, after goodbyes, let it turn inward
toward oblivion and all its power to heal. Earth's beauty
may beguile, but its evanescence is the last lesson to learn.

Foucault Pendulum

Come see the Earth turn.

—Leon Foucault

Knowing by proving is the difference between
science and religion. The world, as opposed
to your world, is moving, though the motion
is unseen, the flow unnoticed, progress made
by miniscule Plank distances (life in between),
and your notion that everything stays in place
is laughable in the face of Fibonacci numbers,
chance, chaos theory, and quantum advance.

Still it moves. Still it loops a little to the right
with every precessive pass. The Coriolis force,
watched for long, can put one in a trance. You
believe in stasis, the staid, stolid-solid Earth
being linear-strong, where all things follow
a straight and narrow path, but you are wrong.

Finding Your Way

Rivers and mountains all empty clarity: there's a road in,
but caught in the dust of this world, I'll never find it again.

—Su Tung-p'o

Any road worthy of travel isn't away from, but toward.
Cluttered cities of clustered people offer entrances
but nary an exit. Every load of baggage begins as
just a want or need. Each hoard of material goods is dust
blocking a door, locking a gate, mocking a minimalist creed
of letting go, giving away, giving way, accepting fate,
emptying mind, surmising "should" from "shouldn't,"
physical gain from the metaphysical "I" refined and rising.

Journey not of this world, though in this world. Rise and walk.
It does not matter where. See before you the ugliest of openings.
Judge not. Clarity could be there. Talk silently with your senses
alone. Let charity be one virtue you hone, honesty one virtue
you own, fortitude one virtue that makes you strong as stone,
and let love, love, be the one sin for which you must atone.

Anchorite

To live in an impure world and be honored
is not a thing my heart delights in:
Rather than by unrighteous means be famous,
I would live poor and keep myself above them.

—Song Yu

All my possessions are dross, and I carry them
as lightly as life will allow, grieving no loss,
refusing to grasp too tightly to material things,
knowing it's thought that gives the mind wings.
Ownership of objects must ever be for naught.

Fame, too, is illusion fed by ego, mortals ever
destined to disappear into the blue, each of us
no more remembered than a snowflake buried
in an unending winter snow, fame being fleeter
than a flash and flicker of lightning's flame.

All of us naked beneath our clothes, all of us
candles in ambient ignorance, all of us to blame
for our illusions of wealth and worth, none of us
awake or aware of our ego that brings us shame,
we seize and tease and please to make our name.

Look at me in poverty. Gaze on my naked mind.
Stare undistractedly for once at my uncaring.
In this moment of having your attention, may I,
not to be unkind, mention your fate is always,
forever, eternally, beyond human apprehension

and that it might not be too late to ask, before
you come to die, what it means to be alive.
Sentient things are everywhere; only mindful
intelligence is rare, existing as it does on a plane
above the senses that search for truth in vain.

Get and grab no more. Release and cease.
Let go. Material you possess cannot be gain,
and your worth in others' eyes will not, cannot
bring you peace. Keep like me. Sleep no more.
Only in unfillable emptiness will you be free.

Here to There Is a Metaphysical Affair

In the palaces above I wonder
what year it is tonight.

—Su Tung-p'o

In the many mansions of the celestial house,
what time is it? In the constellation Orion,
is it ever Tuesday? What weather welcomes
February in the Great Horse Nebula? Grouse
as we will about wee hours' dark, how bright
is noon in the Andromeda Galaxy, M-31?
Are Planck time and length quite the same
elsewhere as they are here orbiting the sun?

What year is it tonight? Without a name,
the year flows apace into human history, but
not natural history. Time and space disappear
without a trace or care, and I, an observing
consciousness only, wonder what markers
measure anything at all in an infinity of sky.

Inner Pattern

Always it irks me—this body not my own.
When can I forget the world's business?

—Su Tung-p'o

Must I dwell in this flesh as if it were me, as if it were
more than a borrowed, outer shell? As if I mesh with
my body's physicalities, as if I found my body home?

My flesh is not a part of me, no more than I'm a part
of my house, my bed, my clothes, my car. Possessions
aren't a part of what people are. Keeping me separate
is an art of which the wise are aware, never confusing
a mundane guise with a haunting metaphysical affair.

If you would truly know me, throw away your senses
and commune with a spot of nothing clothed for a time
in quanta taunting you to come to learn what I am not.

I, like you, am a pure absence now conscious of thought.
I, like you, use my body to swim through a materiality
that is never a part of me, and I, to my knowledge,
did not ask to be. Nevertheless, I, like you, understand
little of how my existence aligns wholly with reality.

When will all this disappear? At death, I'll then shed
this universe as well as this flesh, a fact that gives me
nothing to dread, as I will continue obliviously afresh.

I'll forget the world's bustle and haste and its business
that is, in truth, none of my own, and I will forget my
senses and their entertainment (promiscuous or chaste)
with no sin for which I must atone—come what may,
ready to be disrobed of my atoms and depart this clay.

Metaphysical Lesson №3

Frail and hardly made to last
we crumble away into old age;
touch dry gray hair in grief,
gaze wounded into mirrors.

—Hsieh Ling-yün

All of nature is ambience to our aging,
all of nature a river, a mountain, a sky,
and we are a lifetime yearning to float,
burning to climb, learning to fly. Life
shows us the limitations of our flesh,
how wise it is to embrace our ignorance,
how brave to say goodbye. Each of us
in old age remains a child, everyone
a refugee from oblivion's bliss who
came into being's chaotic froth to either
bathe and bask awhile or thrash about
spasmodically: we decide. And then
space and time subside, party or trial
comes to an end, and all we fought
or played with is put away with sadness
or glee, our presence disappearing
with our opportunity to experience,
to observe, to surmise, to sing, to be.

Invisible Becomes Visible

Lately I've developed a taste for the quiet life.
I think how we could lie and talk together
through the night.

—Su Tung-p'o

Come, Darling, come, and ignore with me
the smug, the smart, the young unkind
who think us out of place and in their way,
who shrink from sitting with us, who mind
our taking our time in line for this or that,
who speak loud enough for us to hear them say,
"Those old fools don't know where they're at,"
and who believe us superfluous in our decay.

Come. Stand up. Take my arm, my sleeve as
we teeter, nothing sweeter nor more heroic as
we wobble a bit unsteadily but firmly on
to wherever we will, we two indivisible, stoic.
Look, Love, how the invisible becomes visible
when we take our time slowly becoming gone.

Thoughts on a Quiet Night

At the foot of my bed the light is so bright
it looks like a layer of frost
lifting my head I gaze at the moon
lying back down I think of home

—Li Bai

I lie awake in a star-bright dark, and moonlight photons
make night day, color white my old blanket, mark me
silently with messages from a satellite slowly pulling away.
Seen from a bed, through a bedroom window looking
onto space and time, infinity can be believed. There it is:
all of its quiet, all of its eternity, all of its startle and awe
sublime for the viewing, and the wise won't be deceived.
I am renewing my acquaintanceship with quantum law.

From my cradle I looked out on such a mystic window
many and many a year ago, and I see again what I saw
first back then, how I, so small a thing here in so small
a place, belong. I am home. I appear. I flower. I fade
after my hour attuned to a universe that became song,
touched me, made me, bade me love with all its power.

Journey

Never arriving, what can we understand,
and always leaving, what's left to explain?

—Su Tung-p'o

Having set out from nowhere, having left oblivion
and all its convenient black, all its sentientless blank,
I don't have a sense of departure or urge for going back
to a state of infinite absence where abysses empty into
nothing, disappearing into nonexistence rank on rank,

nor do I know where I'm going, heading as I am
irresolutely toward death, a state not unlike pre-birth,
dreading those last few hours of pain of dissolution
when I'll wait, hope my stress is brief, and wonder
if my end will equate with my beginning on earth,

for I won't know, I won't know, I'll never know
my origin or my destination, only that I move away
always on a glide to my future and never knowing
why it's so, why the arrow of time is always in the air,
never reaching its target, always having left the bow,

and I am on a journey only, never a visit, never a stay,
ever bound toward a tomorrow that recedes before me,
ever found leaving a memory-mythologized yesterday,
and believing (sometimes in joy, sometimes in sorrow)
that space/time is unfolding as it should, come what may,

and in my hundred-year span, ten-thousand things
have passed me by in their being, non-being flow,
while I observe summers, winters, autumns, springs
cycle, recycle to a point where more observance brings
only the conviction of eternity's eternal come and go,

a froth of quanta, bosons, quarks being, not being,
limning, evanescing in and out of absence to presence,
disappearing to recombine and do it all more and more,
a froth compelling, impelling my participation, elation,
my seeing exit-entrance-exit, every phenomenon a door.

Your Question

. . . a final question, but no words to utter it.

—James Merrill

Let yourself listen to common lilacs' whispered answers
languorous as they are in lazy spring's hazy-azure blue
and harken to their jostling-rustling verbs rousted about
by their heart-shaped leaves minus any emotional actions
of human hue, by wind-tossed inflorescence gone to seed
throughout the summer, by their roots the earth embowers
away from any airy orisons to gods or any sunny creed,
lilac aroma shouting life's last-learned algorithms in your ear.

Let yourself listen to secluded wood thrushes' answers
for though reticent to be seen, they give their evening song
from a base of woodsy brush and force their haunting trill
upon night's rush and trace solitude to its metaphysical source
with a determined will, hidden wood thrushes acquiescing
to be quoted unbidden by the vicissitudes of softening day
as passing light, coming of dew, space/time wending away
toward oblivion's absolution for things done and left undone.

Let yourself listen to inanimate, inorganic matter's answers,
adjectives and adverbs imbedded in silica wedded to stone,
the Big Bang's philosophies laid bare layer by layer for those
able to demystify creation's prose and understand the poetry
of the unknown and how it, too, has libraries of thought
from which universes have grown, from which magically
new laws of physics have come into their own, for you
might find there in a black hole's diaspora all you sought.

Does your question deal with desire? Religiosity? Erotica?
Does it unsettle your slippery lust with love's high viscosity?
Does it meddle in affairs of head or heart, morality's exotica?
Does it divine a purpose to all things under heaven or over hell?
Does it have more to do with you than anything other than you?
Does it weigh heavily in your chest whenever you're alone?
Does it matter if its premise can't be classified as false or true?
It rises from your lifetime spent in the guise of blood and bone.

Life's Circuity

Wanderings of a lifetime—what do they resemble?
A winging swan that touches down on snow-soaked mud.

—Su Tung-p'o

So many beginnings over and over begun again,
so many endings enjoyed or endured, looking back
or looking ahead to life's spirals of ephemera and then
more twists and turns hither and thither, here and there
under no compunction or compulsion, no direction
or accomplishment to declare that bolsters a soul,
back and forth, this way or that until space/time ceases
its leniency, a final resting place, a last traceable goal.

Consciousness wings its way into material matter,
spending its nanosecond of eternity riffling through
the Table of the Elements by way of the five senses
to experience existence with a soft body fated to die,
consciousness flailing when life commences to learn
where on the spectrum of importance its odysseys lie.

Long View

Long have I regretted this life I don't control.
Will I ever stop running errands?

—Su Tung-p'o

My days and years spent tightening and loosening,
getting and disposing, gathering and scattering,
supposing and decomposing, grasping and letting go
distract me from the aging process slowly scrapping
my physical assets and mental resolve, and I know
space and time are out of my control as I devolve
into an old man whose life was measured by others,
my accomplishments not those I would've treasured.

Those days and years, too, held lilac-morning highs,
columbine nights woven of love's touching might,
severities of the five senses overcome by serenities
of the contemplative mind, for consciousness plies
space/time's entangling prose to find the amenities
of life's poetry, and in thickets of brambles, a rose.

Eremite

prayers for a thousand years
conquering winter and defying old age
outlasting the ice and the snow

—Sung Po-jen

Ethereal, ephemeral, my prayers merely wispy things,
 poems more than psalms, psalms more than pleas,
they speak of life's mysteries, the senses' miseries,
and though weak, they are strong in their questionings
of passions that have brought people to their knees
for a thousand years, and I wonder if god or gods
hear in chaotic hurricanes of human angst and fears
what anyone prays, whoever curses, whoever lauds.

My five senses are not me. Tools only, they mislead.
They bring me evidence of this world only, show me
science, leave me alone with all I know. What I am
is apart from this. Belief opens the universe's shell,
faith exposes infinity's door, imagination makes real
eternity's days and hours elsewhere, and all is well.

Love Fate

The moon now so serenely looks upon this earth,
and finds me cool, resigned, like an unruffled well.

—Su Tung-p'o

The moon and I are aged now, even ancient.
We have seen it all: how helter-skelter youth
anticipates a stabbing, grasping adulthood,
how worldly experience precipitates a sure fall
from grace to grabbing, clasping greed.
We're worn out and down before the thorn
of our last decade, broken by ego, torn by need.

The moon watches it all in silent serenity,
passively, nonjudgmentally, only distantly
aware of human activity, human degeneracy,
the moon having no interest in our interests,
in our clutching morality, touching mortality,
the moon sailing a slow circumnavigation
and enduring space/time, ignoring human woe.

The moon finds me cool, I, who long ago
learned resignation, spurned aspiration,
and as a general rule, turned fate into goal.
Amor fati, the Stoics say, and so do I, having
lost belief in a soul, at any rate, and gained
knowledge of my subatomic particles as they
mix and spin to laws energy and matter obey.

Having earned experience's serious wisdom,
having yearned for love and stars in my past,
having tasted, smelled, heard, touched, and seen
this world, I find human angst mysterious
and have put down my five senses to pick up
philosophies more potent, lasting, and serene
to cheer me under the moon's solemn mien.

The indifferent moon looks down, finds me
as you would find me were I here with you,
finds me deepening my very small place
in space/time, spending my days however few
in choosing love, fusing love, perusing love,
my consciousness content to dwell in earth
of its own devising, a deep, unruffled well.

Metaphysical Aspects of Color

I stop to sit for a while, savoring maple forests in late light,
frost-glazed leaves lit reds deeper than any spring blossom.

—Tu Mu

Those with long memories remember spring crocuses' blue,
lime green of new grass, carmine coloring in a sparrow's song,
but at a year's end, white anemones burn like stars, gray bare feet
of youth-shorn elderly shuffle beautifully on cerulean tiles, and it's
not wrong to find artistry in human transience after so many miles.

Look outside and see trees' bright colors aloft deepened, faded,
where shades of decay abide from the soft palette of autumn light,
where yellow and brown will soon dominate the thinning canopy,
where leaves once articulate in expressing life in green language
now go to an ochre and sepia silence before their coming down.

What isn't lovely about a mortal's slow surrender of passion
darkening, deepening through seasons of change and chance,
harkening to steepening age that makes introspection a fashion?
In autumn, who would not find daffodils and forsythia strange?
Who wouldn't turn to asters and witch hazel for a last romance?

True, April is inspiring, aspiring to May with life at its prime,
and the bustling hustle of summer keeps us from looking askance
at fall. Nevertheless, a sugar maple goes to crimson from rose,
scarlet maple to magenta from ruby, everything signaling a call
to deepen, darken our palettes appropriately to honor a close.

Master of None

Resting on a cane, I listen to the murmur of the river
and feel with a pang that I am not master of my own life.

—Su Tung-p'o

Mesmerized by daily business that is ultimately busyness,
hypnotized by glitter of goals tinseled to look like stars,
sidetracked by material ends to the point of dizziness,
desensitized by ego, I've valued distractions wisdom bars.

In old age, I finally pause before this new-found dark
to wonder at it all, how fast it went, this work for a cause
I picked up from others and will now put down for others
and that I advanced not a jot, time exposing all its flaws.

Resting on a cane in the absence of laurels, I stop to hear
the flow of time silent no longer, its hours burbling over
my consciousness, a river in my mind's eye with a will
to go to the universe's end, life within it an errant rover,

and I know myself to have been carried along hapless
and hopeless to a space of reminiscence and rumination
called old age and physical decline, a space by the river
for the elderly who have gainfully learned life's design.

My life has lasted not the length of a song, and its tenor
has been the terribly brief mortality of a human mind,
an ambience to all I've done, right or wrong, and now
I hear in the river's murmur nothing lost, nothing won.

I am not a master. I am not a god. I no longer dance
or play or sing. But I hear and touch and taste and see
physical things not long to be, fear dying, acknowledge
my waste of a life not in my control, a pawn of chance.
But even so, some illusions remain under my control,
and as both the river and I flow and go, I romance
my act of leaving, still believing the world was worth
my time, still deceiving myself that my life from birth
to death could've been memorable, love-filled, sublime.

Metaphysical Lesson №4

I inhabit the constant and wait out the end
content to dwell at ease in all change and loss

—Hsieh Ling-Yün

Ancestors would know me now.
I've shed pride, been shorn of technology
(the tinsel of progress), been shriven
of my doughty innocence by each star
whose hot, rebellious heart has given
truth space and time without ban or bar.

I've learned to trust myself stripped bare,
myself minus whatever other people are,
myself gripped by my own raw longevity
that's allowed me to experience material
existence and watch arrogance from afar.
Naked, I believe. Only clothed do I doubt.

Naked, I conceive. I put the world to rout
by merely waiting silently and alone
with an empty mind, and I relieve stress
by remembering the fate of blood and bone,
the fate of all my kind, and I avoid duress
by riding life's riverine flow unconfined.

Set me down back in the Stone Age, or
place me among ancient, forgotten throngs
and I will love. I will dance. I will know
the existence of the entire universe is still
limned and summed in the romance among
quanta that live and die unseen, unsung.

Loss? What can be lost? Lose? How?
I am the sole inhabitant of myself, I alone.
I'm a metaphysical consciousness, and that's
all that can be known. There's only now.
That's all there ever is, no up or down,
no vice, no sin for which I must atone.

I wait among Edenic lilacs and lilies,
content in my wine and daydreams, happy
as the cirrus clouds encircling Earth, and
I'm as satisfied with death as my ending
as I am with my world beginning at birth.

Metaphysics of Aging

. . . but at the end of this hundred-year life, who isn't a pitiful sight?

—Su Tung-p'o

It depends on the mind's eye, not the body's, for beauty of thought
overawes the senses and lasts after earthly pulchritude comes to naught.
The fine old pine with gnarled and scarred limbs commences to show
its power in its hundredth year, artistry and creativity not being products
of an hour, and the lined face of an elder has ancient eyes with so lovely
a fade they can gaze through the alpha to the omega of space and time.

Anyone becoming sufficiently old achieves a kind of parity with the gods,
a grand beauty that is mortality's last stand before absence empties the stage
with oblivion's ultimate clarity. At the end of any long life, there's
wisdom unachievable by innocence, inconceivable by youth, such is
the disparity between the thoughts of the young and those of the old,
such is the singularity of experience in boldly exposing the bald truth.

Like Shakespeare's Henry V, I say presume not that I am the thing I was,
for my loveliness was more erogenous than numinous, my knowledge
more of matter than of spirit, my passions more aroused by my senses
than by my intellect. All my aging has been to gain a foothold on infinity,
a good beginning to be harvested after death if I read space and time
rightly and understand the basics of clouds and water, rivers and oceans,

ice and snow, if I hear in my oncoming deafness love lightly calling life so,
if I taste in my old mouth everything's serendipity and tang, if I feel
with my arthritic body the oncoming incubator of winter, if I surmise
from all I've learned the ubiquity of love throughout the Big Bang, if I,
in spite of pain, illness, going blind, in spite of loss, can be wise enough
to find within aging's disappearances a terrain where omniscience lies.

Sfumato

Although my body is 70 something, I am 17.

My body is tamed inside space/time, maimed inside space/time,
while my mind roams freely and free, no reason or rhyme
to its flux as it pursues its own fructification,
going where each pregnant thought goes with nothing to lose,
willing to learn at every stage what experience teaches,
my mind my heart's companion in their freedom to choose,
in their rapt adaptation to pleasure and love,
my mind and heart wrapped up in each other's take on metaphysics,
my mind and heart hand in glove,
my mind metaphysical, my heart longing to be,
but only able to know metaphysics through love.

In my last days, I'm curious and would continue on
with or without my body, although I'll miss my heart
that always stood by me furious in my defense
against my five senses that cannot understand my bliss,
and I'll miss, too, my hands that felt flesh's luxuries
and my lips that mastered the vocabulary of a kiss.

My last love is my looking back to my first.
Isn't it true that through all these years
it's been that first love at love's dawn I've nursed?
Surly reality surely falls away into age's dreams
until it's hard to know any difference
between what it was and what it seems.

Time has wasted me, these wracked hands, these lean arms,
and I am not the flesh I once was when I was fresh
and making youthful demands of my body keen with desire,
but I remember everything, and more,
for I've created an alternate history of what went on before:
what we might have been, should have been
if the world we knew had stayed alive although I know
it's only in the trickery of last memories first loves survive.

In life's evening, one muses on life's morning
and all one's awakenings after having been a fetus
moving down a canal to be renamed a baby,
an infant, a toddler, then an adolescent ripening
with innocence inflamed, ready to take erotic measures,
to experience pain and loss, to play and feast
among love's pleasures, to give oneself
engorged with lust to a gorgeous beast,
blurring the line between decency and depravity,
between clean and dirty, between gravity and farce,
between sacred and debased, a teenager keen
to rid oneself of chaste angst, bid one's virginity adieu,
recognizing for oneself that only emotions are true,
that reason is clay, that reality comes into being
when imagination and flesh play at creation
and memory's intimations keep the future fresh.

Raw bliss and ache of that first love have risen to mythology,
nondescript decades placing love on top of lust,
kneading lust into love, needing lust to be love
until I dream of love in awe with tracing fingers
still playing with my mind if no longer my body,
a lover's smile with lips slightly parted reminding me
that great loves sometimes started with guile
before they pressed on to self-sacrifice and then
to expulsion from Eden's blessed isle of reverie and revelry,
ego, id, and libido's false immortalities overthrown.

Even when oblivious, I've known subconsciously
a lover's fingers mucking about in my decades afterward,
obvious we couldn't have gone on bucking tradition
and culture and sentenced to perdition under others' eyes,
yet the tone and timbre, tint and tenor of succeeding years
are a first love's weight upon my space and time,
and that first love is here as my last love, too,
an image imagined, the ambience of our world back then
my ambience now, once 17 in love,
ever 17 at heart and so on, on and on into the blue.

Even when we made love, I knew it would be ending,
and part of making love is knowing grief and loss
wending their way into you, though I did not know
once a moment is past it may last forever
as lust moves from the physical to love in the metaphysical,
and I am awake in my evening with my lover here inside,
lines of our love blurred, lines of space and time
transferred to smudges that make boundaries indefinite
while my imaginings give immortality a few nudges.
Or is it hope that won't let this door close?
Is it hope that lies? Is it hope that's really past love
reappearing in infinite possibility's guise?
The actual answer defies explication in prose.

In my body's evenings, I bend and bow, turn and,
as best I can, remember everything of my morning
opening onto my odyssey of a boy becoming a man,
and the hope of love there at the beginning stays on
in lips that recall kissing, hands that years embolden.
To the quarks and leptons comprising all, I say
we are beholden, for they, in their quantum entanglement,
laugh at space/time conundrums and the chaos where we lie,
and they find an unruly intelligence remarkable that believes
a consciousness that has once loved truly will ever die.

Om

250 billion stars accompany me on my odyssey
to know somewhere in those 250 billion stars
a consciousness like me that perceives itself
to be moving through space/time, flow by flow,
throe by throe, a consciousness like me
that deceives itself by believing its five senses
reveal all there is, its mind's eye revealing
a reality far more appealing to a mortal alive
and afire with Eros and damnation, violence
and love, and so I raise my eyes into night sky
to see a substantiality superior to mortal ways.

The leaden burden of my thoughts succumbs
to suns and worlds aswhirl about a black hole core,
and lambent stars deaden my merely human angst
by their bright silence, their quiet ambience,
and more: their promise of infinity to those of us
who work our way out of religion and myth
and into a metaphysical place that finds us
translating energy and matter into freer minds
that can bear the weight of living and dying,
freer minds that can stare any creator in the face
as its equal, creator and creation of one grace.

The Milky Way and I hold the same view,
the same quantum particles hurling, curling,
twirling tightly about each other inside of us,
the same laws of physics actually affecting us,
the same creative force factually effecting us,
so The Milky Way and I unburden ourselves
by sharing a birth, existence and extinction,
my thoughts flaring up lambent as they do
in those awake to a metaphysical insistence
that we share origin and end, The Milky Way
and I being brothers in this space/time affair.

Sodom

Today would it be as lovely as I remember it?
Shaming Eden, its inflorescence of life burst forth
as I willingly gave away my youth to this place,
my birthright, my first untamed town, game
to try anything once or twice, and I ran amok
over its parks and glades, swam naked in its pools,
played with my fellow citizens, loved in a trice
anyone loving me, and such reverie never fades.

In those days, my body was music, my mind lyric,
and my song rang down neighborhood streets
and ranged over community homes and shops,
waking strong correspondence throughout the town
where our butcher, baker, and candlestick maker
were glad to have me come, loath to have me go,
for I was that kind of child who dispelled despair
as I shed innocence thoroughly, thoroughly aware.

I went to school there, learned between the lines
everything that should be taught but isn't, all about
myself and sexual heritage mine by right of birth,
all about how to deploy the flesh of my body and
its giveaway joy, all about those fresh perspectives
on life available to countrymen who know there's
not a human race but a human family, affectionate
caring being prime, although lust is not a disgrace.

I recall the River Jordan, my body floating nude
in its cold, invigorating baptismal water eddying
my slow way down to the inviting (if misnamed)
Dead Sea, brothers and sisters alive in their bold
mortality beside me, and we sang out hosannas
and psalms of defiance, the throes of youth still
in control of our five senses, all of us generous
in our genesis, all of us in procreative alliance.

I recall redolent gardens of the Cities of the Plain,
rites of sodden spring blossoming through winter's
sullen chastity into summer's flesh-enhanced ways
of renewal, exploration, celebration and praise,
fruits and flowers rising from love we lavished
on them, from life's jollities we shared openly,
triumphal experiences that triumphantly amaze
even now, this far removed from the life we dared.

Our sun rose in spectacular fashion all our days,
the changing moon blessed our behavior, while
all about town in our animal beauty we pranced
in an ignorance that was noble, an indulgence
defying prohibition, and an intelligence justifying
lifestyles spun out of natural tendencies. We danced,
all of us willing to sacrifice wealth and power,
gods and devils, wars and killing, to make love.

Ruled by our hearts, we defied government.
Unafraid of age, we deified long lives dedicated
to the employment of our senses in establishing
what was valuable and what was not, our senses
better for such a task than unimaginative brains
that might lead us into temptation and our creation
of a god-king that would make us thralls in chains
to mythological dogma and dicta religions bring.

When by oneself in bed, one is in a lonely place
that becomes lonelier as years go on. Awkward
to rise alone in the morning, able to talk only
to oneself as if one were communing with a god,
to fix breakfast for one, to leave heart's desires
undone, to keep at a distance those who would
touch, those who would hold, those who would
venture to open a body to let a flower unfold.

Where am I now? How far away have I come,
and what have I achieved? I remember revelries
after work was done, men and women laughing
sinlessly. I should have believed in my body
more than my mind. I've lost the knowledge
a child has of what is good and what is evil. I,
an adult with all an adult's encumbrances, I've
learned what violates the body's truth is a lie.

I will go back when I'm a ghost, although dust
and sand of all that was burned as an offering
is all that remains. Still, my ghost will talk
to broken chards, twisted wreckage, melted clay,
and I will walk among ancestral human ruins
while I say prayers to myself for what was lost,
I, choosing to lie here amid possibilities forgotten,
I, child of physicality, mortal, godless, love-tossed.

Contemporary Antiquities

All time is in the present moment.

—Dante,
The Paradiso

"Once a world power," archeologists say
as they dig, riffle, and sift through artifacts
in ruins of the District of Columbia, U.S.A.

Moldy bones of old congressmen spoil
under weight of broken marble columns
and granite stones where once upon a time
solemn founding fathers envisioned utopia
and thought their thoughts eternal, sublime.

Ages after an atomic apocalypse, archeologists
find America, like Athens, like Rome, to be
rich in refuse that speaks of cultural dystrophy.

Pages upon pages have been written on this:
how miscalculations by a people bring, if not
sudden climactic catastrophe, a slow decline
whereby only art's ghost marks pocked walls.
What was good survives only in art's shrine.

See where technology failed. See where lie
the best efforts of the civilization to survive.
See where die ideologies legions once hailed.

Take this ring in token of my love. Someday
someone evolved beyond us will pick it up
from your dust and say, "Look here, where
still survives this ancient thing, a lonely, worn
remnant still redolent of their wistful lives."

Populist Interregnum

The affairs of men are in turmoil.
The lonely scholar's spirit is vexed.
Why should the melody of the lute
be drowned in the noise of the kettle drum?

—Su Tung-p'o

Poet, you should be alive today to read wrack and ruin
in the trumpets and drums of political orchestrations.
They play with a lack of parts written for cello or lute
as the shallow affairs of men have taken a sad turn
toward stridency and away from fallow, mellow arts.
Men smitten mad with a manufactured *casus belli*
hold sway in government, their narcotic messaging
drugging their millions of minions into being demonic.

Academia gawks at leaders whose talks are presaging
war, conquest, famine, and disease, but academia
does nothing as it watches leaders frighten and derange.
The lonely scholar in his ivory tower may be vexed,
but like the solitary recluse on his emerald mountain,
he must learn to act if he's to counter what comes next.

Preston Clark

How many men can sing about this autumn night?
Tomorrow at sunrise comes the usual round of work,
and this night will seem a dream flight to the moon.

—Su Tung-p'o

You knew and I knew this night would not come again,
but we plunged on anyway, our high school homework
dropped on the floor in the dark, your bedroom door
blocked by a desk chair, our hands groping lust's murk.
You knew and I knew this was not love, but we locked
on sex, panting, sweating, to hell with propriety, to hell
with parents, priests, teachers, cultural sobriety, to swell
with desire, and we tore at each other, just this once afire.

A lifetime has passed. Much calmer, decades have flown
down time's sink hole into eternity, experiences amassed,
many loves, many losses, many mistakes we came to own,
and we are long gone our separate ways, but still, as if
in a dream, I look back to that autumn night in your room
and know, just once and then briefly, we overcame doom.

Metaphysical Lesson №5

we spend our youth awaiting tomorrow
then watch twilight ruins of age close in

—Hsieh Ling-yün

What would youth do? Have it all. Experience.
Be. Exercise all possibilities until they bore.
They would stay young, too, avoiding aging's pall,
ever in their spring of life, never in decline
as forests decline, as gardens decline in dispiriting fall,
ever Adam in Eden, ever Eve before the snake
convinced them both there was something better
and all they had to do was judge to become awake.

Twilight will come. The sun will go down. Night
will show youth darkness, and darkness will show
youth stars. Youth will watch old age closing in,
but those who see clearly with their mind's eye
will remember from their childhood lessons how
a caterpillar's seeming grave produces a butterfly.

Returning Home

The year is drawing to an end.
The leaves are turning golden.
I want to go home.
I want to go home.
I have loitered round the mud flat for too long.

—Su Tung-p'o

In the end of everything, in the end, everything
becomes useless or stale or unprofitable, youth
being a commodity unavailable to those whose
five senses are becoming senseless to the truth
of aging, to the year drawing to an end, to gold
as a funereal color foretelling snow, to news
that a dying year is done with struggling to be
bold in the face of oblivion and pines for rest.

Home? Proverbially, that's where the heart is,
but it's really where memories are, and the test
for locating home is a simple one: recall a face
for which the pulse quickened, time was undone,
and the dark space between you was overthrown.
There's home, even if ghostly in mud and stone.

Safe Arrival

Bell and drum on the south river bank:
home! I wake startled from a dream.

—Su Tung-p'o

Isn't dying the last lap of a journey home?
Imagine it is. It's rounding a bend and there,
always somewhat unexpectedly, what has been
invisible in the space and time you roam
is becoming visible and finally you know.

Throughout your journey, you looked ahead
always aware of an approaching time to go,
your boring, bland days, your exploring ways
ever flirting with goodbyes, always ignoring
that a journey's end is when the traveler dies.

And so you come home again, full cycle,
full circle, the music of your childhood
in your ears, the light in a first lover's eyes
as bright in your creative memory, as real
as on that first morning under Eden's skies,

and so you dream on again, not knowing
the sounds you hear, the light you see
are final particles of your space/time going,
and it's the hour of giving up daily striving to
turn yourself toward oblivion's immensity.

That bell you hear tolls once in your world,
and that drum you hear is your heartbeat
thumping your final, newly useless blood
through a body done and being duly furled
at the end of space/time's outgoing flood,

your river rising, falling, coming at last
to a final turn around which you can't see,
your river shallower than you'd perceived
in your imaginative youth, your salad days
throughout which your mind was deceived.

Your boat of life, your lifeboat docks,
stopped heart, collapsed lungs, flat-lined brain
all testament to your arrival, stopped clocks
signifying a leaving of the plane of the ecliptic
for a new plane minus memory, minus grieving,

home at last, home fast among the flowers
of infinity where an unknown reality is arrayed
before your newly awakening consciousness,
you, no longer afraid, you, newly endowed with
a home surpassing any staid space/time allowed.

Metaphysics of a Poet

I always knew writing meant shabby clothes,
and yet, here I am at death—still a child . . . .

—Meng Chiao

Here I am, my place and rhyme in space and time
running into the blue faster than light can speed,
and yet lullabies sung to me as a child are still
morning songs even in the dawn of my old days.

I concede my body matches patches in my clothes,
and I will admit my flesh is trending chaos-wild
with illness, damage, and wearing out, for those
in mortal life find nothing stays, life death-beguiled.

All of me has half-crossed over the sill of absence,
yet old poetry I used to know lingers at my close
and lullabies heard early then turned to love songs
heard still, sugared arpeggios where love once rose.

Love songs evolving into evening serenades, every
word keeping me young, were easy to sing, and I
stayed a child through my love-making, adult woes
overcome by orgasm's optimism, oblivion denied.

I have written the apocalypse, noun and verb,
in the acts of my life, have lain down in mortality
to rise up wise, and I would love longer, linger
in age's desecration wearing wryly a poet's guise,

a poet's world view that acknowledges nothing
is sacred or profane, and I would leave Eden
not old, never old, but as what I've always been:
writer of a storied story where all in vain is told.

Metaphysical Poets

Abiding by spring and autumn,
trusting to morning and night,
we plow our own fields for food
and coax mulberries into cloth.

—Hsieh Ling-yün

Incomprehensible, unfathomable, unknowable—
they will tell you about it, not in so many words,
but by ellipsis, elision, conceit and pause, by
comparisons of apples and oranges drolly but
dangerously, clause by varnished, burnished clause
until ambiguity clarifies the extent of complication
found in the simplest observation and the concept
under discussion unexpectedly delights and awes,

for the metaphysical poets are not normal—no,
and they ride the alphabet like a Chinese dragon
to bring luck to those deemed intellectually worthy,
bring change to those aching for change and know
greatness is a human chimera and a poem should
produce not "Wow!" in a reader, but "Whoa!"

Speech

Funny—I never could keep my mouth shut;
it gets worse the older I grow.

—Su Tung-p'o

My mind cannot hold a thought, keep it secret,
stash it away as something known only to me,
and so I broadcast my thinking as if it were seed
from a plant bound to die, sending off for free
ideas for others to mull in an hour of need,
thoughts that may germinate in a fertile brain
generations removed, that may flower indeed
long after my mind has moved to another plane.

My loquacity may be reproved by listeners
who can't hear quantum particles speaking,
those who are tone deaf to the atom's arias,
orchestrations of space and time and death
that are an ineffable ambience for my words
revealing a metaphysical purpose for breath.

Tao Te Ching

All created things
are like a dream an illusion a bubble
a shadow a dewdrop or lightning.
View them all as this.

—Su Tung-p'o

All created things are dreams, illusions,
bubbles, shadows, dewdrops, lightning
that flickers jagged streaks crookedly
across emptiness our minds call the sky.

Yet the mind seeks in a ragged somewhere
a permanence in science and a reason why
it exists, what impermanence really is,
and if any creator is able to hear its cry.

Such a dream! Such an illusion! Bubble!
Viewed as what they are, they're beautiful
and worthy of delusion, much trouble,
a futile attempt to touch a face of a god.

View the cosmos out of the Land of Goshen
making its slow way into the Land of Nod,
the mind's miracle of imagination creating
the uncreated visibly and invisibly flawed.

In the risibly fake bliss of material reality,
in the insubstantial sublimity of the world,
remember this: the five senses lie. Being
in space/time is one long ethereal sigh.

Find what you love. Take it to heart.
Embrace what you hold as worthy
of embracing and let go as dross all else,
for all is nothing and all gain is loss.

Floating along on your flow of seasons,
watch for eternity, awaken to infinity,
your journey into awe without beginning
or meaning or ending or reasons or law.

Ghost

Very deep is the well of the past.
Should we not call it bottomless?

—Thomas Mann

Never to come again, this evening darkens,
backyard birds, once garrulous, now in roost,
sweet smell of neatly mown grass strong
in an almost still air, crickets one by one
starting to say, "Here I am," starting to ask,
"Where are you?" and I am riding along,
turning with massive Earth slowly, inevitably
toward its someday annihilation and my own.

My grandmother's home-made unsweetened
lemonade stays tart on my tongue, and I sense
even back there in that ever-unappreciated Eden
I'll never be able to make it this way when grown,
and I take another sip, absently knowing my sips
are numbered, stars half-heartedly coming out
in this not-quite dusk as the sun dips below
my sight-line, night coming on unencumbered.

As my young uncle smiles his handsome smile,
as my mother quietly rests her girlish head
on my father's boyish shoulder, as a retriever
brings laughter to my cousins as he chases
and nips at fireflies now beginning to rise,
as dark blue replaces amethyst, as an old deceiver
moon plies her way up the far side of heaven,
I half see a bit of eternity in a moment's guise.

I was only a child, and many a day lay ahead
that I would remember with more emotion,
and now, this steeped in years, this filled with
a full life's actions and reactions as an end nears,
what notion causes me to recall a minor night
so long ago? Where has it been, this memory,
all these decades of accumulating encumbrance,
coming back to me here in cold and snow?

Little memory, why are you here? Who are you?
Once, when I was briefly like the others, I sang,
then moved on, went away, disappeared into life
while partially remembering things that never were.
Little memory, you fall quietly into consciousness
and recur. I smile at my propensity to be sad over
recalled love, to reboot stalled time when I was glad
and rode to sleep in arms one time sublime awhile.

As long ago as then, I didn't want anything to end,
the somnolent dark deepening to inevitable night,
neighbors shuffling home, relatives going in,
my young, warm father carrying my dozing body,
my drowsy, cozy soul inside to bed and further
childish dreams. Couldn't the hour have lingered?
The moon have waited? What reason now has this
bit of thought to disturb my mature themes?

A cousin soon leans in. He has caught a firefly.
He shows me flashes of light held in his hands,
and I hear my pretty aunt cry, "Shooting star!" and
sure enough, one courses through ink-black sky.
I am drowsy. I would sleep. I am dropping off
out of the blue into apocalypse. The retriever turns,
barks once, eyes me nodding to infinity. He comes
for me from across the lawn. He is coming still.

Metaphysical Lesson №6

I meet sky, unable to soar among clouds
face a river, all those depths beyond me

—Hsieh Ling-yün

I'm kept by my body's matter from seeing what matters
to my mind. But as flesh toils, spoils, and falls away,
I'm spirited outward toward ultimate epiphanies as aging
scatters the lies of my senses, fantasies of achievement,
myths of progress, old beliefs that have had too much sway.

Elderly, I meet sky and see for the first time it's bottomless.
I face life's river and cast myself naked into last possibilities.
I'll never soar. I'll never understand. I'll never climb
indefatigably over obstructions of my senses' observances
to find my serenity in eternity or fulfillment in the sublime.

My time as me is almost done, but I'm not going away,
nor will I pine for sensuous victories hard-fought and won.
My future is not with you, nor is my attention on your stay
this side of fruition. Rather, I will ride by without notice
celestially, quantumly, secularly—as ever, my own guide.

I always existed until I fell into flesh, this blinding me
with five unnecessary senses to flail and splash about
in an ocean of quanta, finding me baggaged with a body
that agonizes and tenses over a mundane space/time thing,
I, alive, inside this beast that must sob and feel and cling

to mortality as if it were real, and I am brainwashed, too,
as if I will not be released at the body's death, I, pining
for insubstantial, worldly goals, whining about financial,
social, political ephemera in life's hot and frothy brew,
forgetting very early on what I am and what I am not.

Incarnate, now old, now lame, now experienced in being,
I consent to the universe's temporary law. I wait alone,
greeting each day without power to hold it still, seeing
space/time fly by with some degree of awe, feeling yet
I have a bit of free will, using it to keep me from regret.

Mourning Gomorrah

Lot beheld the whole Jordan plain to be well-watered
like the Garden of Eden, and this was before the Lord
destroyed Sodom and Gomorrah.

—Genesis 13:10

42 thousand in Hamburg, 29 thousand in Dresden,
200 thousand die in Hiroshima and Nagasaki,
fire and brimstone (a hell that had been unseen since
an asteroid wiped out dinosaurs) fell by human ire,
and that doesn't count the mayhem and the maimed,
the 3rd degree burns, the injuries, the suffering
of those blamed and blistered in war's purgatories,
not to mention a hate-inflamed annihilation of Eden.

Where are all of the lovers now? I remember them
in their spectacular nakedness on banks of rivers
from Jordan to Styx, from Mississippi to Rhone,
from Columbia to Ganges, Amazon to Murray,
Danube to Yangtze as they flow on to mix in seas
where sailors know pride and power are overthrown.

When I was young and there, I knew love in flower
and walked with lovers and worshipped lovers
in a secluded wood hidden by an occluded moon,
on secluded beaches, my bare body on sand or stone,
my body doing what love has bidden late or soon
surrounded by plant and animal kingdoms doing
the same, compounded by urges making bodies game
to try mastering flesh in passions both wild and tame.

The gods were jealous of our flesh's five senses,
our sexual athleticism whenever two of us shared
ourselves and paired off, for there were no dicta or
dogmatic fences separating us from our proclivities
to match and mix and mate, no religions, no laws,
no dry interdictions by some sly authoritarian state.

We would go back home to the time before gods,
when we splashed Scotch whiskey on naked parts
and licked and sucked it off, when lovers fed
each other mouth to mouth following the prods
of their own desires, loving with nothing to dread,
running riot with arousal through city streets
with sunlight glinting off sweat and marbled stone,
lust's feats tinting our wet skin with a red blush.

How happy we were, alone among a garden's hush
to fend for ourselves without need for obedience
to anything other than youth in a time of no laws,
never fearing such time so soft so soon hardens,
never knowing despair wading in living's shallows
where daily life sang sex with no need for pardons.

Do you remember the city's darkness at midnight?
What else mattered besides your five senses alive
and detecting, selecting, interacting, protracting
with another set of five senses, both of you light
in a metaphysical world starved for it, both of you
ablaze with the consciousness the Big Bang carved,
both of you set to amaze space/time with creation
set to your own rhythm, your own personal rhyme.

My countrymen, have you lost your memory of
our beautiful pornographies of the body and mind?
Holy scriptures placed strictures on human bliss,
deciding who can have it, who must do without,
barren chastity absurdly unnecessary and unkind,
an implacable shaming colliding with a human kiss.

42 thousand in Hamburg, 29 thousand in Dresden,
200 thousand die in Hiroshima and Nagasaki,
and have they taught us nothing? Who would not
if they could, slacken if not abandon laws of state
creating radioactive waste, laws that blacken lust
that given a chance would free humanity from hate
and build bridges, tear down walls, invigorate trust.
Let humans sate themselves with flesh, not dust.

Where once green was, now a world of worn brown
spreads over leveled lands once keen with promise.
Where once there was blue, now lie waters that drown
hope of youth's orgasmic, orgiastic ecstasies that once
flourished in a city on a human plane, one nourished
by love's civilization before its innocence was slain.

Tao Time

After all, what's ten years
when a thousand pass like hail on the wind?

—Su Tung-p'o

Or for that matter, what's a lifetime?
Even if it's yours? Did you think to flatter
yourself with worldly importance? Or
to experience with five senses the sublime?

You will not be remembered, nor will I.
Like finite hail in an infinite wind, decades
pelt down frozen again and again and die,
all our mindful imaginings to no avail.

They pass through your open arms, years
unaffected by your attempted embrace,
years by the millions, billions, trillions
here, then disappearing without a trace.

What do you recall of your bland years?
What acts of your hours, let alone days,
do you remember from any of them?
In the pelting hail of years, nothing stays.

What of them all would you grasp? Joy?
Really, what specific joy can you recall?
You are not Alexander at Gaugamela, nor
Achilles with Patroclus at the gates of Troy.

Can you remember acts of making love,
the details of which were nourishing rain
to your body's thirst, memories of which
were fated to become faded, abraded, slain?

After all, what are years that you should
notice their eternal hailing, storming fall?
Wrap protective philosophies about you
as your flailing body goes grieving it all.

Flowing with Rivers into Oceans

Tumult, weeping, many new ghosts.
Heartbroken, aging, alone, I sing to myself.

—Du Fu

And when I sing to myself, aging and alone, again
I hear ice cubes clinking, crinkling in crystal glasses,
lads and lasses' young laughter giving my pulse a thrill,
and I realize once more how red all those roses are still,
how blue the lilacs, how blue the lake, how blue the sky,
how real yesterday stays, and my mind does a double-take
as my body drops decades along dusty ways of space/time,
and common sense and logic and reason do not know why,
but I once more smell honeysuckle and spiced cologne,
touch his arm, his face, as imaginative memory takes me
to a place where old ghosts greet new ghosts strong
in their affirmation of the beauty of all that's flown past,
yesterday spliced to now, yesterday somehow here again
in my longing song, my mind grown to fill the cosmos,
my caged and closing world becoming less unkind,
my aged and decomposing world becoming redefined
as a remembrance of fleshy Eden now autumn-tossed,
luxurious leaves once defiantly green now red-embossed,
woods where we once lay unseen now arrayed in frost,
tumult and weeping replacing the sexual hijinks and cheer
that once endowed all loves, whether ordained or star-crossed,
that once saw us greet rough lusts eager and unbowed,
and heartbroken at unrecoverable health and youth lost,
gone hoarse in my unremitting solitude, wan in my aging,

I accept and I sing a swan song belonging only to those
whose moment in space/time is long in the tooth, departing
being the only theme that has my interest, knowing as I do
that death is starting, is a starting point, is a beginning
that erases distances, collapses eons, and in its coming
releases consciousnesses from obligations to five senses,
increases awareness of oblivion's beauty, decreases
unfairness of the laws of physics as I even now sing
in the boyish baritone I once used to charm many loves,
sing at least in my mind's eye, hearing in my mind's ear
the testament of love sung back to me, silent many a year.

Tender Mercy

Suddenly rain came from heaven three inches deep.
The Creator's mercy is beyond comprehension.

—Su Tung-p'o

Is an ultimate consciousness conscious of us
and, if so, does it have a conscience? More likely,
in its infinite existence, it's unaware of our fuss
and fuming and cares, we who last less than
Planck time and who fashion sycophantic prayers.

Not beyond comprehension are the complexities
and impacts an ultimate consciousness would cause
by any single act. An ultimate consciousness
might pause before the fact of disturbing the universe
if it were aware of how we misconstrue natural laws.

What ultimate consciousness dares to chance our
extinction by flood, fire, freezing, or disease, or
end our affairs by conquest, war, famine, or death?
If it knows of our existence, wouldn't it rather be
worshipped than deprive us of our pitiable breath?

Or is an ultimate consciousness ultimately wise?
Does it let us founder or thrive in accordance with
cosmic whims in the guise of subatomic particles,
allowing us to survive or perish indifferently, we,
brief, mortal creatures, too prone to grief to cherish?

Not beyond comprehension are the complexities
of ultimate consciousness. Not beyond redemption
is the living chaff of a universe's far-flung worlds
if that ultimate consciousness develops sensory
organs, ethics, judgment, and becomes forgiving.

Turning Away

Tired of seeking new beauties in the company of youth,
I sit facing the palace flower and recognize its old fragrance.

—Su Tung-p'o

As I age, I move slowly from seeking to waiting
wholly focused on tasting, touching once again
old beauties now fully sating my newly frail desire
in evening to raise love above youthful, erotic fire.

Let youth hasten busily on. Time will chasten.
I have no doubt youth will learn that new beauties
have little worth, coming in, going out, unless
they have a worth youth's too callow to discern.

I sit facing a palace of memories, recognizing
the lilacs of then in the aroma of lilacs of now,
and I sit in the bracing recall of house-high lilacs,
beauties somehow enduring my aging's pall.

Paths from where I've been to where I am
are strewn with loveliness left behind
and the narrowing, harrowing paths ahead
promise few new beauties to my way of mind.

Still, as I've left the hunt for new beauties
so sought after by boys and girls everywhere,
I've left boys and girls behind as well,
new joys from new toys no longer my affair.

Look at this old photograph. See? There
among other sepia days and hours long gone
are beauties that come back, stay with me
now lighting darkening descent as I travel on.

Metaphysical Crickets

Just as what is truly seen is seen in the mind's eye,
so what is truly heard is heard in the mind's ear,
and in between life's arias and wails come snippets
of sound forming a background to sane and absurd
worldly music and noise, chirrups often ignored
in the quotidian cacophony of the spoken word,
chirps often mistaken for random phonetic quanta
bouncing off an ear drum, meaningless, broken,

but supine in a summer meadow on a hot night,
on one's back in the dark, in the grass, pausing
inconsequentially with much of life still to pass,
hear them now, those chirps and chirrups, saying
there's more that should entertain a mind than
industry, accomplishment, space/time, praying.

Waves and Hills

The shimmering waves are translucent when it clears.
The mist-veiled hills are transcendent when it rains.

—Su Tung-p'o

The shimmering, skittering days of summer, so shallow
in their content, really, reflect only the light of youth,
deflect from their surfaces any apparent aging and allow
celebrants of summer's superficialities to dodge the truth.

It's okay. Be young. Being young is a classic ballet,
so seize its shimmering moments and grand jeté your way
across life's June, July, and August stage to land clear
into coming autumn where time has made you a sage,

and you'll come to see what were once precious joys
were only rapidly passing translucent waves of hours
that floated you onward and out of transparent youth
and into an opaque age foreign to summer's bowers

of light living, living love, loving youth's brief might
and ascendancy that by September is ready to descend
into fall's night of living chaste as both body and mind
wend slowly to shimmering snows of winter's waste.

But you, by then, are above remorse. What remains
after veiling mists of youth and its busyness depart
is a new understanding of what space/time is about:
hills of experience behind a now-transcendent heart.

Wine in Time, Time in Wine

Only in wine is man himself,
his mind a cave empty of doubt.

—Su Tung-p'o

Wine in time, time in wine, they go well together
swimming, mixing with each other to flow cheerily
through the mind's cave, a fine Merlot fixing
broken hours, a heavy Malbec and heady Médoc
consigned to spend eternity nixing human fears
as calendars awash with Cabernets pass kindly
into oblivion, wine and time seeing mortality out,
wine and time inextricably linked to the end of doubt.

The mind's cave has a rogue river running through it,
cold time's river, old wine's river going from a child's
golden vineyard to be poured into experience's bottles
for succor, stupor, and intoxication through life's wilds
where time binds and wine throttles mind's evasion,
man himself floating on both toward ultimate negation.

Metaphysical Lesson №7

Embracing change, the mind never tires,
and gazing deep, our love for things grows.

—Hsieh Ling-yün

Chasing reality, the mind looks here and there,
never tiring from one discovery to the next
as it finds itself tracing patterns of space/time
against a backdrop of oblivion from which
everything came, because of which everything
is worth the same. The mind eventually will
embrace anything, given its propensity to create
worlds of complication, then avoid the blame.

But the mind gazes profoundly, fondly,
and though everything it conjures is a fable,
it has as both its raison d'etre and salvation
its capacity to love, able to find in chaos
something wordless, unexplainable, worth
the world, the sorrow, the lie, the stars above.

Horology of Trees

Taking no note of our calendars and clocks,
they dote instead on the way imperceptible seasons
move with space/time toward hinterlands forever,
and a pendulum's sway is as meaningless to them
as the slow inevitability of an hourglass's sands
that drop day after day out of every life's endeavor.

They grow tall into infinity's lazy somnolence,
into the universal drowsiness of atmosphere and sky.
They flow through all changes from the Big Bang
to an eventual stopping of the spin of the last proton
when leptons and quarks collapse and histories die,
growing tall regardless of the fate of every photon.

They dwell apart from our obsessive measurements
from Planck time to eternity, and they do not fear
an accumulation of another annual ring that closes
the cycle of another immaterial, immemorial year,
preferring the natural, boundary-less analogue
to humanity's unnatural, discrete digital veneer.

Their chlorophyll biographies are written hourless
in every spring, and their seeds in summer ignore
career schedules of human young and bring cheer
of a delicate making to the human old before
autumn turns leaves garnet and gold in pre-winter
ritual celebrating how grandly infinity draws near.

They take the time to let time go. They know.
They know. In dust and duff their roots cling
to manufacture dreams dark and warm against
a chaste and chastising snow ever coming down,
and their roots gather nutrients and holy water
to salve a consciousness ignorant of renown.

They remember. Their memories are twisted
in their towering crowns, xylem and phloem
keeping their cambium's promise and passion
beneath their protecting bark, all ills resisted,
all time unnecessary, all time merely the present
in perpetuity as they flourish in our ambient dark.

Winter Into Spring, and Vice Versa

A spring night hour is worth a ton of gold:
the pure scent of flowers, the moon's pale light . . . .

—Su Tung-p'o

Even when eighty, spring night hours are heady,
heavy with the sincerities of a thousand flowers
that you may not see again for a long while,
not until a summer, an autumn, and a winter
of oblivion have come, lived and gone on
leaving your body to its detriment and detritus,
breaking you forever of the illusions of youth,
waking you to infusions of mortality's truth.

But even at eighty, spring night hours are gold,
regardless of how much time has flowed beneath
the bridge of life taking you from young to old,
for to new roses, a new moon, you will bequeath,
as all else closes, your wisdom gained from cold
winters survived and winters returning so soon.

Yield of the Mind

Thorns grow in the field of the mind;
clear them and there's no finer place.

—Su Tung-p'o

In the field of vision of the mind's eye
there grow such gardens of lust and play
one wonders if the real world we ply
with our five senses is where we'd stay
given the chance to live in the mind alone
where fruits of our hormonal excitement
hold sway, where roots of our libido's goals
are sunk deep in our cerebellum's fantasies
and give rise to our humid bodies' wiles
that trick and trap and brutalize, demonize,
fetishize as we move through mortal trials.

Better to be blind. Wisdom needs no light,
needs no touch, smell, taste, hearing, nor sight,
and in an empty field of the mind, space/time
does not exist, is no impediment to being,
has no worth with no dimensions besides self,
and seeing as we know nothing before birth
or what happens to us after death, space/time
is an interlude of happenstance and chaos
dependent wholly on heartbeats and breath,
dependent on our minds to give it meaning,
our minds immaterial, immortal, transcendent.

The field of the mind gives us our life's terrain.
The shield of the mind protects us from taking
to heart what others judge sacred or profane.
The yield of the mind is winnowed experience,
wisdom that remains after uncoupling pointless
flesh from ourselves, yield of the mind being
what's left over when death curbs gain with loss,
yield of the mind being what stays when death's
curfew draws our day's curtain, leaving us alone
within ourselves and what we know for certain:
It was brief, our time spent in blood and bone.

Mirabile Dictu

I follow a twisting path to a secluded place,
a meditation hall surrounded by flowering woods.
The mountain light stirs the delighted birds.
My heart is as empty as this reflecting pool.

—Chang Jian

Alone and slow on a low road around a cold pond,
knowing snow to soon uphold winter's dolorous tone,
I feel declinations to the bone, and my mind's eye
and my heart respond as autumn dies its annual death,
autumn saying goodbye, autumn of which I've grown
so fond, red and bronze leaves, russet and tan needles,
wind rustling every rust-brown sword fern frond littering
literal and figurative paths twining and indivisible
leading from today into invisible space/time beyond,
and I am on an odyssey from which I will not return
to what I was, my innocence dissolved in the acid of
experience, my early life evolved into consciousness
while my flesh revolved uselessly about five senses
until my observations resolved themselves into wisdom.

Ill and old, I look skyward, out beyond the biosphere
onto the plane of the ecliptic to see a pattern of migration
of souls into interstellar space, into imagination, into
death, which is only the animate becoming inanimate
in a universe without pain, without time, without place,
an eternity of flowering quarks and leptons, starlight
stirring the delightful elements of the Periodic Table
as I become oblivion, empty as ever, infinite as ever,
present as ever in the history of having been, mystery
of having been alive, present as ever as a twisting heart
in a secluded place following love and following night
into foreclosure and out of it again leaving no mark,
for if we truly love the power of life, power of light,
then we of sweet mortality must also embrace the dark.

Lazarus

At their desks, these first-year wonders wait,
fresh from summer, still with bits of clinging Mom and Dad
not wiped clean from their new free will,
at their desks and eager, fresh, even dew-eyed,
appealing in their powerful innocence,
their bodies supple, lovely to look at and imagine feeling.

And I, their first professor, am about to speak,
to tell them everything. Unlike Prufrock, I am Prince Hamlet,
even Virgil, in my own way, leading young Dantes downward
to self-recognition, to easy virtue, to a latent dismay
with how hard sin is and how it has begun, this moralizing,
marginalized sophistry the aged give as alternative for fun.

The blond in the first row, his clear eyes big,
his lips sucking an eraser he won't need,
is ready to take notes. Ankles crossed, he leans forward
wanting to know, wanting to understand this time.
His high school platitudes behind him, he wants college truth,
his cheeks flushing with anticipation of my first word,
his back braced, his mind cleared of parental detritus,
ready now to really learn what's real and what isn't.

The brunette in the first row leans back, breasts pushing out
for no good reason, for none of the others can see her front
and they're wasted on me, as are her liquid limbs that move
smoothly through her blouse sleeves, her small feet and dainty hands
that are out of place in what I have to say, and she shakes her head
gracefully, her dark curls gently bobbing as she settles herself
to finally hear, to hear it all told boldly and well by the odd professor
who, to her, looks like a withered corpse and not at all like the blond
sitting beside her who has yet to notice all of her that I've noticed.

They look at me, the two of them, ready to welcome like the others
wisdom from wizened professors who look nothing like the living
who even now sit in the Student Union scoffing at strictures and dicta
and homework assignments that clash in the night with human arousal.
Tell them of Homer? But how? Shall I tell them how long ago
all they haven't yet imagined came to nothing?

And I have come forth out from my tomb-like room, summoned.
By whom? And to what purpose? By students, of course,
who've paid their fees and demand knowledge. By students
who think they can be taught everything. But I in my white lab coat
wound about me like a tight-fitting shroud, I with my chalk about to turn
and write my name on the board beneath course number and date,
I must disappoint, must tell them—not in so many words—
that what's worth learning cannot be taught. It sits without language
on the lips of the dead. It lies heavy in lore lost in the Big Bang.

So I have been over on the other side and now come back to tell you
in thoughtless language you cannot speak,
in mathematics beyond your powers of calculation,
in delicate artistry whose least tracings defy your crabbed hand,
in music you mistake for noise
and with infinite grief you can't begin to understand.

Last Years on the River

With night about to end and a light wind on the water
I'm leaving in my sampan
to spend my last years on the river.

—Su Tung-p'o

I'm leaving my comfort zone, pain a companion
if I let it accompany my thoughts, otherwise
I'm on my own as I push off from youth and lust,
leaving in the guise of a philosopher, recluse,
and life's unrequited lover toward distance just
the other side of all Hubble Telescope sighted when
it opened onto ontological arguments with stars
as metaphors for all experiences beyond existence.

With life about to end, and a light wind upon me,
I am afloat as never before, and I wend my way
on my river of swirls and eddies as I near the sea
only metaphysicians know, so I send back goodbye
to remembered loves so long a part of me as I aged
that now I feel no heartache at my having to go.

Finding Mr. Watts, My Former High School English Teacher, Gone

Under the pines, I ask the boy;
he says: "My Master's gone to gather herbs.
I only know he's on this mountain,
but the clouds are too deep to know where."

—Chia Tao

Far removed from my youth's antiquities, I had wandered back,
briefly wading time's shallow river past previous life, previous grief
to find again an estuary that had nurtured me momentarily
before the unstoppable current plunges me on into forgetting again
what once was forgotten before a word, a line, a recalled belief
woke me once more to what once had been my innocence before

everything was different. Nothing had been left unchanged,
the town now a city, the streets once few now multitudinous,
and people upon people bumping, clumping, ignoring, hurrying,
in the way and not finding the way, people on top of people,
none of whom I knew or knew worth knowing scurrying by,
and I stood at an old address I knew before my life went awry.

"He's retired, you know," an elderly lady said answering the door,
what must have been a grandson bracing her, hand on her arm,
and he smiled at me for no good reason other than thinking me
like his grandfather an old fellow meaning no harm, and before
I could speak, he added, "In winter season, he's usually gone
to the library's stacks to explore, forgetting evening coming on."

"I'm sorry you've missed him," the frail woman said, but I,
in my mind's eye, hadn't missed him at all: I'd found him
tramping along on the narrowest part of his journey through
space/time still learning, still yearning for wisdom's emptiness,
still speculating on nothingness from which all things grew,
still burning with metaphysical fire lighting his way into the blue.

Death of Su Tung-p'o—July 28, 1101

Vital spirit has an existence independent of the body,
and moves without dependence upon material force.
There before one was born, it does not vanish after death.

—Su Tung-p'o

The spirit enters flesh knowing, but once in, forgets.
Once it's in, the five senses begin their sophistries
weaving a life like a skein of hypnotic florets,
blossoming experiences that bloom and fade
one after another from callow youth to hollow age,
none lasting long, none casting shadow nor shade
on the immaterial spirit nothing has made.

The body is heir to incompetence, incontinence,
petulance, and temerity. The body is there to give
the spirit cause to reflect on passion and to live
learning the way before light returns to dark and flaws
of mortality become self-evident in the dissolutions
of temporal worlds, of institutions, of beliefs, of goals
that come to an end in old wounds, regrets, and griefs.

I am done with appurtenances of fleshy pleasure,
seeing nonexistence through the aperture of existence,
done with things material, let alone things imperial,
and I am shedding this body as a snake its skin,
as a butterfly its cocoon, as a cicada its shell.
In the nurturing darkness of a new moon, I am borne
aloft into eternal nothing as clear as a temple bell.

Memorial, Washington State Ferry

"Your attention, please," the mate's voice says,
"we are slowing a moment for a memorial,"
and sure enough we all do, all of us, even those
entangled in a bustle to get to the other side,
restless chunks of festering business waiting,
little urgencies pricking us into a stressed huff.
Below on the car deck a small group slowly forms,
and a mate lowers a rope, beckons them forward,
the ferry engines slowing whatever our hurry,
and we all are coasting together on a rainy sea.

A heavy-set woman unwraps a nondescript urn
from a carefully held towel, handing it in turn
to an ungainly boy, a shy girl, an older man,
and she watches as each tips the urn to scatter
dust into a windy vortex off the ferry's stern,
a fine grey mist streaming over the roiled wake
in a high breeze before settling, disappearing
into grey oblivion of sea, sky, and late afternoon.

As the ferry's horn sounds three long blasts,
the four bow heads. The woman hesitates,
hides her face a moment in the towel, kisses
each of her party, and shakes the mate's hand.
He speaks, his words lost to us in sea sounds
and engines, then looks up to the bridge, waves,
and the small group, holding hands, rejoins
some two hundred of us who have in silence
watched this mini-delay in our grey crossing.
The ferry's engines begin their normal thrum
to push us forward again against a grey sea
and under a low, grey sky, where a fine dust
disappeared, and white seagulls rise and cry.

Biographical Note for Su Tung-p'o

One of China's greatest poets, Su Tung-p'o (1037–1101) was a government official during the reign of the Sung dynasty (960–1279). After achieving some success in the Sung bureaucracy, he had the temerity to criticize some of his superiors' new policies in his poetry and essays. This resulted in his arrest, exile, and then constant assignments to distant provinces as a form of banishment. During this time, his view of life and poetry underwent significant changes as he became a more reflective and introspective person. His poems written during this period have a distinct metaphysical and stoic cast to them as he meditated on life's vicissitudes, the worth of family and friends, the flow of time, and the inevitability of loss. Finally, after being exiled to Hainan Island in the South China Sea, Su Tung-p'o was fully pardoned and asked to return to government service in the capital. He died on his journey there.

A thoroughly captivating biography of Su Tung-p'o is *The Gay Genius: The Life and Times of Su Tungpo* by Lin Yutang and published by The John Day Company of New York in 1947.

The best selection of Su Tung-p'o's poetry for the English reader is *Selected Poems of Su Tung-p'o*, translated by Burton Watson and published by Copper Canyon Press of Port Townsend, Washington, in 1994.

A wistful, poignant search of Su Tung-p'o's old haunts in modern China can be found in Bill Porter's excellent *Finding Them Gone: Visiting China's Poets of the Past*, published by Copper Canyon Press of Port Townsend, Washington, in 2016, pages 215–225.

Biographical Note for Rob Jacques

Rob Jacques was raised in northern New England, graduating from both Salem State University and the University of New Hampshire. He served as an officer in the U.S. Navy during the Vietnam Era, and he has taught literature courses at Northern Virginia Community College, Olympic College, and the United States Naval Academy. His poetry appears in regional and national journals, including *Prairie Schooner*, *Atlanta Review*, *American Literary Review*, *The Healing Muse*, *Poet Lore*, and *Assaracus*. *War Poet*, published by Sibling Rivalry Press in 2017, is a collection of his poems related to his experiences while on active duty in the U.S. Navy. Having completed a civilian career as a technical editor/writer for the U.S. Navy and the U.S. Department of Energy, Jacques lives on a rural island in Washington State's Puget Sound. Strongly influenced by the works of Emily Dickinson, Robert Frost, and James Merrill, his poems explore metaphysical aspects of life and love as well as paradoxes that arise as flesh and consciousness move together through space and time.

Acknowledgments

The following poems first appeared in the indicated journals:
Invisible Becomes Visible—*The Healing Muse*
Recluse—*Flint Hills Review*
Lazarus—*Assaracus*
Memorial, Washington State Ferry—*Cascade*

CPSIA information can be obtained
at www.ICGtesting.com
Printed in the USA
FSHW011246081219
64692FS